Shiela K Clark

Author and illustrator based on the
Isle of Man.

Dedication

This book is dedicated to the memory of my Mum, who was the inspiration behind Bertha, my Grandmother and my Nana.

Also by Sheila K Clark

The Magical Rainbow Garden Series:
The Magical Rainbow Garden
The Naughty Mouse
Poor Miss Quirky (coming soon)

Acknowledgments

I would like to thank my family and friends for their support, Claire for her work on the illustrations and all of you for supporting my stories by reading my books.

Meeka Manx Moon

There is a place not far away, where fairies work and play.
It has a wonderful waterfall where the fairies like to feel the spray of the water on their faces.

This is a story about one fairy called Bertha, a very unusual name for a fairy, but she loved her name as much as she loved looking after the wildflowers and creatures of Waterfall Glen.

Bertha had a heart of gold and her dream was to own her very own pair of shoes.

When Bertha told her friend Joy, she laughed and pointed out that her feet were too small for shoes and besides fairies don't walk, they fly.

"I will go to the Fairy Queen, I'm sure she will be able to cast one of her magical spells and give me a pair of shoes. Will you come with me?" asked Bertha.
"Of course I will, but why do you want a pair of shoes so much?" replied Joy.

"I have watched how the little human children dance and I need a pair of shoes like theirs to be able to dance just like them" Bertha answered.

"It's too late to go now, we can go tomorrow after we have done our work in Waterfall Glen" said Joy.
"What a good idea" replied Bertha happily.

Bright and early the next morning, after all of their jobs were done, Bertha and Joy set off to see the Fairy Queen.

This Fairy Queen did not have a castle instead she was happy in her little mushroom cottage with her pet beetle. When Bertha and Joy arrived, the Fairy Queen was outside talking to her flowers in the sunshine.

She noticed Bertha and Joy flying up the path and smiled at them. "Hello lovely little fairies, what can I do for you on this beautiful day?" asked the Fairy Queen kindly.

"I wonder, Fairy Queen, if you might possibly use your magic to give me a pair of shoes?" asked Bertha.

"How unusual, fairies do not need to wear shoes in Waterfall Glen. I will grant you a pair for one week. After one week, if you still want a pair, I will ask the shoe pixie to make your very own pair. However, there is one condition. When I grant you a pair of shoes you will not be able to fly, as shoes are for walking!"

Joy looked at Bertha and said,"Do you really want a pair of shoes even if you are not able to fly?"
"Of course I do!" Bertha replied with a smile on her face.

"So be it," said the Fairy Queen and used her magic to give Bertha an enchanted pair of shoes.

"Oh Joy, look at my lovely shoes! See how they sparkle and they even have a little pink flower, my favourite colour! Thank you so much Fairy Queen!"

Happy in her new shoes, Bertha was about to fly back to Waterfall Glen with Joy, but when she tried her wings did not work. In all the excitement she had forgotten she could not fly! So she started to walk.

"I will see you back at Waterfall Glen, it's going to take a while for you to get home!" said Joy.

Bertha waved her friend goodbye and could not stop smiling as she set off home.

Bertha's smiles did not last long as her feet quickly began to get sore and hot. She felt she had been walking a very long way, even though she had hardly gone far.

She decided to take a rest under a tree, when she noticed a little speckled egg lying on the soft grass.

"Oh dear, it must have fallen from the nest and I can't fly up to the nest to take it back to its mother!" Bertha cried in dismay. She began to try and think of something she could do.

"I know" she said to herself. "My feet are really hot. I will take my shoes off and put the egg in one shoe, then cover it with the other to keep it safe."

Bertha looked down at her sore feet and was glad that they were on the shaded, soft grass to keep cool. Soon a bird flew down beside her, looking worried.

"Have you seen an egg? All my babies have hatched and one is missing! I think it must have fallen out of the nest!" cried the bird.

"Don't worry,"" Bertha replied. "I have put the egg in my shoe to keep warm and safe."

Suddenly there was a tweeting sound, Bertha lifted the shoe and to her surprise there was a little fluffy chick. Bertha was so happy that she was able to help the mother bird, who thanked Bertha for her kindness as she happily took her chick back up to her nest.

"Well, that was lucky I had my shoes! Now let's see if I can get them back on." But Bertha's feet were so big and swollen she couldn't get the shoes back on.

"Maybe I can fly now I have no shoes on" she thought, but it was hopeless as she tried and tried without success.

"Oh well. I'll look on the bright side, I helped a chick with the shoes, even if I can't wear them" she smiled to herself.

Bertha started walking again, this time carrying her shoes. In the distance she saw her friend Joy, flying towards her and carrying a box.

"I have brought you a blanket, some food and water as it's taking you so long to travel and you're not even halfway home yet! Why haven't you got your shoes on?" remarked Joy.

With tears in her eyes Bertha cried that her feet were so sore and that she couldn't get her shoes back on.

"Well, maybe now you have no shoes on you can fly!" said Joy.

"I tried but it doesn't work," said a sad Bertha, wiping the tears away.

 "Oh dear. I'm sorry but I have to get back to work" said Joy looking at her friend's sad face. She gave Bertha a big hug, said goodbye and reluctantly flew off back to Waterfall Glen.

After Bertha had eaten and tided up. She decided to put her shoes in the box with the blanket and began to make her way home again.

As she was walking Bertha heard the sound of crying near the stream that flows from Waterfall Glen. As she walked closer, she spotted two baby butterflies.

"What's wrong?" asked Bertha.

"We have been playing in the water and our wings are so wet we cannot fly home" said one butterfly, "we are so cold" said the other one.

"I will ask the flower nearby if I can borrow two of her fallen leaves, I'll put one in each shoe for you both to sit on and dry off" Bertha offered kindly. "When you feel dry enough to fly, I can give water caught in the leaves to the flower for her to drink."

Soon the baby butterflies were feeling a lot warmer and dry, they thanked Bertha and happily flew back to their home.

Bertha carried her shoes to the flower and took each leaf out of her shoe gently and offered them to the flower, who drank the cool clear water and thanked her for being so kind.

Bertha decided to try the shoes on again, but it wasn't long before they hurt again and she had to take them off.

She could finally see Waterfall Glen in the distance though, and started to smile. "It shouldn't take me long now," she thought hopefully.

Suddenly she heard her name. It was a grasshopper who was beside her, "I heard you had a pair of shoes, why are you not wearing them Bertha?" asked the grasshopper.

"My feet hurt and I can't get them back on" she replied.

"Oh, I'm sorry to hear that Bertha. But since you have two spare shoes could you possibly carry me in one of them as I seem to have lost my hop. My friends are waiting for me near Waterfall Glen if you are going that way."

"Of course I will!" replied Bertha who quickly cupped her hands and placed the grasshopper in one of her shoes.

A little further down the road, the grasshopper spotted his friends and thanked Bertha for the ride, remarking that her shoes had become very useful. They both laughed and waved goodbye to each other as Bertha put her shoe back in the box.

Bertha's eyes lit up as she saw just how close she was to Waterfall Glen. She put down her box and ran as fast as she could. All she wanted to do was sit under the waterfall and feel the cool spray on her sore feet.

Joy had spotted her friend running towards the waterfall and shouted over to her. "Where are your shoes?!"

"In the box you gave me," Bertha said from under the waterfall. "I am going back to the Fairy Queen tomorrow, my feet are hurting so much." Bertha told her friend with a look of sadness on her small lovely face.

"You can't," said Joy "You were told to wear them for a week." "I will not be able to fly for a whole week, and I can't wear the shoes" replied Bertha. "I must go back tomorrow. I'm so tired."

Bertha picked up her box, gave her friend a hug and went into her home between the rocks and fell into a long and peaceful sleep on her bed of leaves.

The next morning, as the sun was shining brightly upon Waterfall Glen, Bertha made her way to Joy's home to see if she would come with her to see the Fairy Queen.

Joy was happy to help her friend, and offered to take over Bertha's daily tasks so Bertha could start the long journey by foot. Bertha was so grateful and set off waving goodbye to her friend. It would be easy for Joy to catch up with her as she could fly quicker than Bertha could walk.

As Bertha was walking, she started to think about her shoes and how she hadn't been able to walk, let alone dance. This thought made her sad. Her thoughts soon turned to the little bird and the baby butterflies and how she'd helped them, and when she started to think about the grasshopper who lost his hop she could not stop laughing. It hadn't all been bad.

Joy soon caught up to Bertha. "We haven't far to go, look there's the Queen's cottage!" Bertha shouted up to her.

The Fairy Queen was sitting outside in her garden and noticed Bertha walking with no shoes on her feet with Joy flying beside her.

"You're back early, it hasn't been a week yet," commented The Fairy Queen.

"I am so sorry," said Bertha almost in tears, "I can't wear these shoes any longer, they hurt my feet so much."

"Remind me why you wanted a pair of shoes," the queen said to Bertha.

"So that I can dance like the human children" she answered. "Joy, come and stand next to me so Bertha can show us how the human children dance. I'd like to see it," encouraged The Fairy Queen kindly.

Bertha did as the queen said and started to dance with a huge smile on her face. She spun around with grace, waving her arms as her feet moved quickly. When Bertha finished The Fairy Queen was smiling at her.

"You see Bertha, you did not need a pair of shoes to dance - you dance beautifully without shoes! I have been told how your shoes were useful for helping some of the creatures you met on the way back to Waterfall Glen. Since you do not need shoes to dance, I will let you fly again and there will be no more talk of shoes."

Bertha was only too pleased to agree. "Remember Bertha," said the Fairy Queen, "Waterfall Glen fairies don't need to wear shoes. They fly, not walk!"

Bertha thanked the Fairy Queen and with a smile on her face flew away beside Joy, feeling so happy and lucky that she could fly again.

As for the shoes, they were indeed very useful! The Fairy Queen used Bertha's shoes as little plant pots which she placed in her beautiful garden for all to admire.

The End.

Printed in Great Britain
by Amazon

18496996R00025